D1564841

IN THIS HOUSE

HOWARD ALTMANN

In This House

TURTLE POINT PRESS

NEW YORK

2010

ISBN 978-1-933527-33-8
Library of Congress Control Number 2009929505

Cover photograph by Aaron Siskind, *Ironwork, New York City,* 1947
© Aaron Siskind Foundation

Design and composition by
Wilsted & Taylor Publishing Services

CONTENTS

IN THIS HOUSE

Sounds

A man may read a poem
to write a poem.
He may make love
to find love.
He may climb a mountain
to transcend a shadow.
He may forget the years
to retrieve a day.

In the assembly of life's acts
a man searches for his parts.
He walks in the rain
to touch the veil of childhood.
He waits for the sky to break,
for a wound to close.
He smiles at a stranger
to let the unknown pass.

And when sleep eludes him
it is not darkness that captures him.
It is the years at the window
throwing light in his eyes.

It is the ascension of shadows
dissolving from his frame.
It is love's ephemeral body
trusting what is absent.

Then a man may write a poem
to read a poem. To her.
When she is finished listening
her silence will begin to drop its sounds.
The way rain does not hurry
to cover all that is ground.
The way a horizon gradually recovers
from the passing of a train.

Bluebird

A swirl of leaves tosses its bag of colors
over the shoulder of an unmarked road.
In the century-old barn where the leaves
take refuge, the wind is a permanent resident
rehearsing the music of abandonment.
And in this hollow the leaves—who found
each other before they got lost and braided—
are endlessly tweaking the quartet of clapboard
walls, while midnight gusts sweep notes
through the cracks, forcing the leaves
to break down into ontological refrains—
The order of things is the disorder of a life;
evolution does not arrange its strife.
The arc of a spirit is a rainbow in the dark;
the finest arc does not leave its mark.
Yet in dawn's nest it is just one note feeding
off another, where horses once had their say.
One could almost hear the bluebird whispering
to the blue sky: when I fall out of view
it is not because of you.

Island

The moment one says it is a moment
of perfection, it is something less
than perfection. So on the island
of Fernando de Noronha, I will be quiet
now. I will let the birds speak
Portuguese. I will let the waters speak
dialects of green. I will let the rocks
tell me I was never really born;
and the vistas carry my insights
to an early death. I will let the breeze
nudge my years off one cliff here
and one cliff there. I will let the air
confiscate my passport. And I will let
the sand send my battles to the sea.
Let them all simply make an island
out of me. The moment I say I am lost
without love, I will be something less
than lost.

History

It is Budapest
and the December light
is lost in the dark
of the morning fog
and memory is trying to lift its weight
from the river Danube
to that basin
history has watered down.
It is the fog
tired of being

above it all.
Follow me, it says,
we don't have to commit
to the land or its people.
We can make love to the earth
and leave its bed alone.
We can roll over headstones
and no one will know
the names of the dead.

We can slow the movement of horses
and pass their fear
back to time.
We are all in exile.

II

When he was a young man
at Auschwitz
my father leapt out of line
for a potato
and was saved by a bell
that never rang.
Sixty years later he stands
in his place
by his mother's tomb—
the only tomb—containing
his hunger for memory.
Feed me! Feed me!—
he does not cry;
like the ground does not cry
1944 from its spring;
and the horses
clocking the cemetery walls do not cry
for the fog to deepen.
Only a congregation of birds
hovering in Talmudic chatter

tolls the silence—
as a distant river's passage
rolls over the frozen limbs
of winter.

What they learned
before they fluttered out of formation
and what they looked like
in full flight
and whether the birds ever return
to pay homage
are simply questions that remain.
Never far from home.

Composition

If I could tell
the story of my life
it would be the branch
drawing its tree
on the hard wet sand.
It would be the man stopping
to erase the tide
from his mind.
It would be the waves
sealing his shadow
with all the changes
only the clouds could bring.

And if someone else could tell
the story of my life
it would be the poem
I never wrote
from a book of poems
I never opened
whose page was missing

once all the leaves had gathered
on the porch to listen.
It would be the man stopping
to adjust his posture
on the abandoned road.

Transformations

Frightened of the next life
being exactly like this life
he asked to be a bird
so he could hide in the trees
at night
and not be alone.

Someone must have heard
his cry
and before he had no more
lift in his being
an old willow offered him her weight
so he could feel light

again.
The birds that knew him
from his long walks
accepted him like he was
one from the nest,
though what plagued him

as a man
was not a fear of heights

or sudden descents into the void.
Do not follow me
he pleaded to that self.
Despite unending gyrations

he could not eject the part
that parted him
from the earth.
Resigned that it would live
through another death
he simply let himself fall

to her window
from where he had stood one night
and asked to be a man
again;
to reveal his heart to the morning
that had not broken.

Salvador da Bahia

One cannot deny the role of the sea
In lighting the color of the sky.
One cannot deny the role of the sky
In lighting the surface of our imagination.
One cannot deny the role of fiction
In lighting the reality of our days.
And one cannot deny the role of the days
In lighting the strata of our darkness.
But one can deny the role of darkness
In lighting the color of the sea.
As one can deny the role of shadows
In lighting a lynching beneath a tree.

After Dark

I am the boy who returns
to the same whore
in the same foreign country;
I am that man.

I am the boy who runs
from the same truth
with the same mask;
I am that man.

I am the boy who asks
for the same love
from the same woman;
I am that man.

I am the boy who empties
the same body of water
with its same body of reflections;
I am that man.

I am the boy who enters
the same rooms with the same windows.

And the one who sleeps in the same bed with the
same light;
I am that man, I am that man.

I am the boy who leaves
the same echo
with different voices;
I am that boy, I am that boy.

The Death of Curiosity

Then came the death of curiosity.

It was sudden and it was quick.

Many did not see it coming.

It woke up one morning and couldn't move its face away from itself.

Narcissus would have gilded its frame.

An actor would have leaned in for a lesson.

A mime would have surrendered.

Painters and sculptors would have gathered their instruments.

Children would have tried to make it laugh.

But curiosity was alone in its death as no one knew that it had died.

Politicians graced it in speeches.

Scientists alluded to it in private conversations.

Neighbors greeted it on Sundays.

Crowds assumed it was in their laps.

All the while curiosity was at capacity.

It had what it had.

And it would have no more.

Then came the death of the country.

It was not sudden and it was not quick.

Few did not see it coming.

It woke up one morning and unhinged itself.

It did not leave a piece of land or a body of water.
It did not leave a flag.
It left no memory of soaring spacecraft or landing men.
There were no museums to document its descent.
There were no old maps to study.
Even the wars that never really died had no more blood to go
    around.
Human and beast alike hovered in the air.
Yet there was nothing bird-like about them.
They were not leaves ushered by the wind into the great
    hallways of time.
They were still human and they were still beast.
That simply had no ground to stand on.
The feet of trees wiggled their ankles in the air.
Buildings that stood up to the sky sat unmoored from their
    foundations.

Then came the death of surrealism.
It was slow and it was painful.
And no one saw it coming.
If it woke up one morning not a soul could say.
Its oxygen was reality and its history of ailments.
The supply of raw materials to manipulate had exhausted
    itself.
The shape of things had simply depleted the inventory of
    possible contortions.
Imagined forms were confined to the unconscious universe.
Floating in the horizon with animals and plants

Painters and sculptors lost all perspective.
No politician could claim chaos as a constituent.
No chemist could conduct an experiment.
The ink of philosophers had no medium to wander.
The dissolution of gestures gave actors nothing to mime.
Narcissus could not reflect upon her reflections.
Children could not fix their laughter.
The world could not place its fears.

Venice Beach, 2008

And I'm listening to Mendelssohn's piano concerto
a kite's distance from the ocean and there's a bottle
of ketchup and enough orange marmalade for a family
of twelve next to my elbow and I'm feeling older
than my years and herein lies what I'm being told
to write by the Academy of Important Poets who take
their toast buttered with 18th-century symphonies
and string quartets that float out to sea in a Claude Monet
as the milk stands by the salt but the pepper is forlorn
and the Formica is the truth and truth is a word.

Where have you gone, Walt Whitman?
Come have breakfast with me now.

The Long Flight

I am a maple leaf
    on Abe Lincoln's nose
        in a European park.
Raised on milk and god
    I drank snow at night
        and watered the grass in June.
The radio plays in two rooms
    as I listen to the music
        that will die in one.
Clouds continue to anchor
    all those distant places
        floating deep inside.
And birds will come to arrest me
    as I capture their flight
        to release my own.
But tracking that ephemeral line
    between will and will be
        draws the water's edge.
Only when an old man stands
    does a slight limp let me know
        the earth is not going anywhere.

Who am I in this world
        of infinite identity
               and finite breath.
The unraveled helix may be a plane
        yet plain life remains
               twisted till the end.
When I was a boy kicking stones
        that old metaphor—a bunch of ants!—
               was largely in the dark.
Was it light
        that sent the smallest
               scurrying for cover.
Was it premonition
        that inched me closer
               to their panic.
Was it the world at my feet
        that had no need
               for moving things.
Was it the poem's first constitution
        bereft of country and of man
               in full regalia.
Or was it the distant sea
        flagging down the uniform
               steadying me for the wind.

A Public Trial

Will the inventor of language please stand.
Raise your right hand. Do you solemnly swear?

Please sit down. And cross your legs.
Fold your arms. Focus now on the white
Point on the white sheet on the white wall.
Continue until further notice.

Will the inventor of language kindly tell us what he sees.
Will the inventor of language maintain his focus.

Ladies and gentlemen, you are herein given notice
That the inventor of language has moved his eye.
May I ask the inventor of language to step forward.
May I ask the inventor of language to tell us what he saw.
      May I ask the inventor of language to tell us
          What he saw. And why he moved his eye.

For the last time I ask the inventor of language to tell us what he saw.

Contempt carries a lifetime sentence
Of solitary confinement;

Day from night and night from day
Will not light the years.

The inventor of language will be released
One day before his death. On that day a white cloud will fall
To the ground. From this cloud will emerge a plume of red hats—
One for every man, woman, and child, worn in honor
Of the inventor's death. The inventor of language will be buried
With a red hat. The day after his death all red hats will be swept
Off the floor of the earth into the mouth of the rising red sun.
That night the moon will cross its legs and fold its arms,
      And aim its white light to the buried red hat;
           For the world to see.

In This House

In this house that is not mine
I can hear a home
knocking at a door
left unlocked for years
only the days knew to come
and go as they please.
At the top of some ridge
it has found me
with my walls
building solitude out of trees.
At the nadir of some work
it is trying to enter
and show me to my room.
And at the middle of life
it is throwing stones
as if there were a window
night could open
and I shall see that figure
reaching for light.

I was born in a crowded room
and before the age of reading

I excused myself from the story
and closed the book.
Now there is a story of a mountain
in this house that is not mine
and it stands half-read.
Now there is a story of a river
and it throws off half-pages here
and half-pages there.
And there is a story of myself—
my lies flowing from half-truths
whose full narration I can't wind down.
But when the wind turns the lake
into Braille for the half-standing trees
I retain some kind of vision
of nature:
Mother, I was a scribe in Egypt
in that house that was not ours.

The Axis of Being

In the absence of moonlight
the mind shapes a moon
in its depiction of night.
From incompleteness
it leans on a circle
for the self to go round;
and in her absence
I searched for another
to make that sound.

In the presence of sunlight
the mind scatters shade
in its reading of day.
From over saturation
it hungers for a spot
for the self to rest;
and in her presence
loneliness followed
her every crest.

In the fleeting twilight
the mind carries shadows
over the dunes.

Dandelions

The man who invented the breeze was happily married
to the woman who discovered the wind. They bore
no children and they had no pets. They lived on a hill
overlooking a meadow of wildflowers. When spring
came the man congratulated his wife and the woman
congratulated her husband. When all the blooming came
and went and October began spilling gray, neither faulted
the other for the landscape that showed no memory
of friends or neighbors. But inside the man always believed
the wind was to blame and inside the woman always
believed it was a succession of small breezes that was

at the root of all the deflowering—though neither said
a word in this direction for many years. When November
was spilling quiet and the last blue heron had written
itself out of the sky, the man turned to his wife
and gently inquired—*Had I not invented the breeze
do you think the wind would ever have come?*
Without a pause she replied—*The breeze is a bereft child
that has never evolved from its protean state.* The
brisk outside air hushed itself inside and the tension
that grew between husband and wife stretched the bones

of silence. But when the bruising was all said and done
and January began spilling white, neither faulted the other
for the landscape that had now burrowed its way
into the house. The house that bore neither children
nor pets now ceded all evidence of life but for the elderly
couple who moved about like barren trees on an
empty stage. The roof and windows were all
that protected their frail beings. And they held each other
at night to lend anchor to all that remained: themselves.
As February began spilling storms and icicles
the inventor of the breeze and the discoverer of the wind
were sculpted into a white figure by a blizzard.

Not until spring returned, spilling green, did the frozen
embrace of husband and wife melt itself and dissolve
into the air. Lime shoots shot themselves out
of dead grass where a dining table with candlesticks
had once stood, reaching for the shafts of light spring
now splintered through the roof. And when all the
blooming came and went, purple cornflowers and prairie
sunflowers stood defiant. The brutal winter
that followed preceded a modest spring where a sea
of common dandelions waved from the meadow,
beyond the windows of the empty house.

Stones

I would like to be a stone.
By the side of a road.
On a roadless island.
Of no interest to man.
Of no curiosity to animals.
Invisible to birds.

I would like to step out of my stone.
And be another stone.
On the other side of the road.
Prized by man.
Of solace to animals.
A spot for birds.

And on my stone
both stones, please.

Yielding

There are days you just want
to plant a tree
and know that in a hundred years
what was rooted in your being
that afternoon the years collapsed
is still not finished
extending itself to the universe.
Let nature speak

for the unspoken, you say.
Let all that you've poured
into your stand
take the earth's grasp,
away from you.
Let the measure of your life
branch forth
with the imprecision of your hands,

soiled and true.
The cypress, the sequoia, the common oak—
they live longer than us
for a reason, you say—

let it fall to the leaves
to break down.
Let it fall to the seasons
to lift the darkness

from the ground.
Let it not be words
you reach for, you say—
where the trees stand
far from man
is a silence the snow sits and reads;
whatever they exchange will always remain
buried beneath our feet.

The Painted Room

And you wait. And you wait.
And you say you're not waiting.
It is living that you're living.
Candles light a room. Two shadows darken one.
The bread is warm and the moon drinks from your cup.
You travel in and out of books.
The plants are green.

And you wait. And you wait.
And you say you're not waiting.
It is new experiences that you're experiencing.
A sky takes your jump. An ocean floor takes your gaze.
Substances are passed and matters pass away.
You move in and out of awareness.
The language is foreign.

And you wait. And you wait.
And you say you're not waiting.
It is the seed that you're seeding.
Children are schooled. The dead are mourned.
The foundation hardens and the voices recede.
You wander in and out of helplessness.
The interior has a face.

And you wait. And you wait.

And you say you're not waiting.

It is the emptiness that is emptying.

The catatonic stand at the bus stop. The lonely sit at the
    night cafe.

The other is homeless and the other is without.

You do not wander in and out of the rain.

You do not wait for spring.

Fragments

An old man with a new hat
is running out of pride.
I want to tell the truth
but I don't know how.
The wind is our best pen
and it blows poetry out of the water.

I wait for days and weeks to enter
a feeling that's had years to leave.
The ocean keeps throwing questions
it has all the answers to.
A candle lights a room
and dims the stars.

When all that consoled consoles no longer
loneliness finds a room inside the one it knows.
I am shrinking from the light
and turning into space.
An old man with a new hat
wears his smile in the dark.

The History Teacher

When she could no longer speak
she smiled long enough
for the silence to quiet down
and adjust its chair.
If it had her wheels
the silence would have moved
infinitely closer
to her finite breath
and brought her to the peak
of memory
where words forget reasons
for talking themselves
down.

When she could no longer wave
her arms amid the green
of the Berkshire trees
to greet a visitor that Sunday in July
she smiled long enough
for the landscape to quiet down
and adjust its row of pines.
If they had her nature

the pines would have released themselves
from their bark
as if they too wanted to hold
whatever was human
up to the world.

And when she could no longer move
us past the edges of her pine box
the sound of the shovels
lasted long enough
for the years to quiet down
and every class she ever taught
to rise.

Animals

It happened in broad daylight.
A museum of world renown was exhibiting
the facts on behalf of the people when
animals stole their way past the absurdists
and the realists with the acclaimed collection.
Disagreement persists as to which animal
is now running with the facts and whether
the perpetrator is the ultimate beneficiary.
If collusion among the species was at play,
one could say the entire kingdom is up for grabs.
If it were one beast acting on its own accord,
friends and family have not come forward
with any clues. On one matter, however,
a consensus remains: the facts will never be
the same. To say they are being dragged
through the mud would be an oversimplification.
To argue that they are being chewed to pieces
suggests that they could be broken down.
And to assume they could even be held
in the jaws of one callous creature is simply grist
for the mill. The reality is that most people
never viewed the facts when they were mounted

or before they were purchased by a family trust
for an undisclosed sum. Only a privileged
few actually held the facts in their hands;
and they are all deceased. While a visit
to their burial sites has been recommended
by a committee of volunteers, access
has been denied, as the pursuit of the facts
has been deemed to be no spiritual matter. And
though roads, bridges, and tunnels have been
sealed off, conventional wisdom has determined
that whatever four-legged species committed
the crime, it is now a flock of birds careening
out of control with the weight of biblical dimension
crushing its wings. Thus all bodies of water
have been summoned back to land, and all
clouds and patches of blue sky are passing through
routine inspection. What has emerged
is a kind of dinosaur that, without the constitution
to breathe in another medium, will not survive.
And so fact-checkers, the world over, have since
been caught lying on their backs, holding
their breath; for this time to pass.

Olinda

I am the old woman in the old town,
the stone face in the stone window,
the eye on the dog and its two eyes on the bird,
one day following another,
one day that knows no other.

Once I was a man in a manly town,
the cold face in the cold window,
the eye on the dollar and its two eyes on the bird,
one day following another,
one day that knew every other.

Neither tells the truth, of course,
as bold colors are never meant to
in cobblestoned Olinda,
where sugar men once stretched their canvas,
where Brazilian women now spread their lace.

But this morning the banana leaves took the rain
like drum skin that doesn't give in
to the anger of a man—
just to his nature of tapping
on all that cannot be said.

Central Station

And when I leave
one place for another
I am at that place
that has never left me
all my life.
It is in these corridors
that darkness and light
eke out a living
based on nothing
but my moves.
Sit with me for a moment
and I'll show you
the photographer's dilemma
in black and white.
Here on the river's mirror
is a house of clouds;
I am trying to float
to the ground.
There in the sunken valley
is a gathering of horses;
I am trying to climb
into my picture of freedom.
And right through my mind

swim these words
as they try to reach out
of the train
and beyond the window
that captured them.
Now walk with me
into the crowded station
and notice the face
of anonymity
and its body of change.
Now let's stand long enough
to observe the unending stream
of people leaving one place
for another.
At this central station
in my life
it seems I must stay
in one spot
to be known.

Shoes

What is it about old shoes
that pulls a string or two—a gentle
puppeteer's tug between the eyes
and the heart—as if it were our
vital signs that were hanging
in the attic. Surely that torn pair
of faded blue jeans and tattered red
party dress will send us running back—
yet they don't walk right inside
the body the way an old pair of shoes
with their deepest wrinkles free
of dust paint the air with particles
of time. And I choose to understand
this now after all those shoes
in Washington were collected and
displayed, a rubble of lives exhumed,
shipped by plane over icy waters—
tagged and photographed and positioned
under the scrutiny of donated light—
lending torsos and limbs and hands
to the eyes and hearts that stopped
behind the double-sided museum glass.

And I choose to understand this now
after seeing the eyes of my father stop
behind the refracted pane, his concentration
uncamped by the curated heap,
his eighty-year-old vision now
a child's running through the mud—
every old man's shoes his father's and
every young girl's shoes his sister's—
and the past was never buried
or exhumed, simply strung to a staged
presence, hanging like a heart
in its chambers that was blindly
beating life to death.

November Wound

i don't know the names of trees.
or the names of flowers—i don't know
the names of rivers or lakes or rocks or
snakes. i don't even know the names of towns
i pass that tell me their names—

i know when the sun is trying its best
to change our light. and when the clouds mean no harm.
i can separate the hay that's been cut
from the hay that's still cutting shadows.
i can point to the horses ready to be crowned.
and I can tell you the names of friends
who have waited.

but I don't know the names of birds
or the names of the founding fathers, or
the names of the teachers who introduced me
to the founding fathers. i wish i could say
i know the names of the explorers who discovered
this land. and maybe a few of the names
of those who died defending it.
or the names of some of the species
the centuries have buried—

it is monday
and i couldn't even tell you the name
i gave to last monday, or the monday before that.
and so on and so forth.
i am out of names. i am all
out of names. i am even out of names for her.

it seems there are to be no capital letters today.
only small letters. small single letters.
some piled on each other
like hospital beds without wheels.
some bleeding their colors into the dark
blanket. some caught between two winds.

it is that time of year
and all the leaves have landed.

Words

We miss what we miss.
In adulthood, we miss childhood.
In January, we miss July.
In the city, we miss the country.
In the desert, we ask for clouds.

We miss what we miss.
With one view, we miss another.
With one memory, another speaks.
With one desire, another whispers.
With one night, others are lit.

We miss what we miss.
When it passes, it stays.
When it feeds, its hunger grows.
When it fills, it empties.
When it matures, it loses age.

We miss what we miss.
To what we miss, years.
To how we miss, seconds.
To where we miss, timelessness.
To why we miss, the end of time.

We miss what we miss.
And in all the missing, a life.
And in the life, a mourning.
And in the mourning, a story.
And in the story, words.

A Man Walks Through

A man walks through an open field
reading epitaphs in the odd passing
of a cloud. The soil is parched, the distant
hills are gauzed, the air is defeated:
winners all, the man believes. Even
the sunken summer sky holds its own
medals, he maintains, casting forth
from bronze to gold with blithe
indifference. Language, good heavens,
inside the house is another house
still, and here roams his foundation,
a blade of grass dangling from his lips;
a seed in the horizon's mouth.

And as he steps into the vastness,
as one would step into the vastness
of an ocean, that takes the mold of body
and being, asking for nothing
in return, gravity becomes his to lose.
In this way, he is nature now, and all
that is human is observed:
the fragile formations, the territorial claims,

the unspoken need; the earth
digging in its heels. The landscape
thus arrested, he wants to stay the execution
of time; and let the universe judge
his brief few words.

But nothing comes. Only night. Animals' hands
and pockets of cold air. Civilization throwing
its weight behind all those stars. Bent, he
straightens a bed into the ground, and all that
is nature becomes the mind: the invisible
transformations, the fantastical machinations,
the irrepressible truths. From these depths
he remembers how he was once an angel
in the snow when the sun affirmed: *you are*
an angel in the snow. He recalls how he was once
an airplane in the house when the house affirmed:
you are an airplane in the house. Then his eyes
begin to close, as the field closes in; and in.

ONE MAN CANNOT ESCAPE THE WORLD.

Inside Her Studio

A spoon in a glass
is also a tulip in a vase
when one is patient
with the light.
It is a groom in a chapel
the night before
when one imagines a parent
exchanging vows.
It is a tree in a bowl
of heavenly snow
children are drawn to
after a storm.
And today
it is a kind of friend
to the still life
I cannot brush away—
see how the spoon
appears out of thin air
in the clenched fist
of my mother

as she listens with a glass
through the walls
of my father's rooms.
Notice how this memory stands
at funereal attention
for the passing of all
that has passed
before me.

II

Inside her studio
the blank canvases stood waiting
for us to let go.
As I mapped her world
of solitary spoons
inside empty glasses—
her dead parents were standing
there in my mind.
It was the year she escaped
from her country and I escaped
into other people—when New York
had artists who escaped
into tin-ceiling lofts.
When we would cross each other
near the flickering streetlamp
occasionally our shadows touched

and settled;
while the darkness stirred.
Looking back I still see
the universe marrying us
to its cold hands;
drinking us whole.

Sunday Monday

Now you know everything.
I opened the window
and all my air
fell off the ledge
into your chest.
You turned it over
in your bed of thoughts
and combed through it
for something to keep.
You kept these words.
To yourself.
And returned to my door.
We stood at the window.
We sat out the silence
with silence.
We watched Sunday leave.

Gravity

The poem breaks down.
The day's architecture collapses.
I am walking over words.
The longing
for a hurricane of emotion
to sweep the mind
frames the body;
I am made of sand.

Neither blue sky nor blue ocean
tells the story
at the end of the horizon
when all that floats
is a fiction of the eye.
Beyond the beyond
imagination and knowledge
finally come to shore.

Identity is a bastard child;
the parent of all tides.
It is the color of water
hiding in the rose.

It is time's thorns rounded in the hourglass.
But when I turn it all upside down
I see the gravity of it all;
the sentences that were once falling down on me.

Field

It has sealed its windows and removed its signs—
religion has shut its doors without further notice.
Prayers from around the world have breathed
their last breath. Some have asserted disbelief
in the believers. Others have conceded disbelief
in themselves. Many have complained of mismanagement
and abuse. Almost all have pled centuries of exhaustion.
Prayers in every language have severed their every tie.
They want to go home. They wish to return
to their places of birth and gestation. They too wish
to sing the story of their survival. Yet not a pair of hands
that held a prayer could be recalled. Or a solitary voice
that passed through a prayer identified. Not a birth
or a death could be summoned. And so the prayers
have detached themselves from their bindings
and their books. They have let the wind dictate their fate.
And they have withered like November leaves. But not all.
Some have remained—landing on the heads of angry
worshippers whose fury at the prayers could hardly be
contained. And these prayers have burrowed themselves
into each of their temples. They have morphed
into appendages weighing down their bodies. And now
there is no extracting the prayers from the minds

of the angry. Nor is there any remedy for the myriad
of infections developing and spreading from one believer
to the next. And so the faithful have been herded
into houses of worship long abandoned. And under
one roof angry worshippers of all faiths sighed their last
sigh. And under one roof prayers that had parted
with their every word to the rain and the snow
and the daily habits of man now touch the wordless—one
body brushing up against the other—waiting for a pair
of hands to hold it; a voice to claim it.

Nature

If one returns all the ink
from the poem
to its source,
the page is white,
the cartridge is full,
and the mind cannot erase its envy.

If one returns all the blood
from the ground
to the fallen,
the earth is innocent,
the bodies are guilty,
and the heart cannot live with reason.

If one returns all the water
from the river
to the mountain,
the valley is barren,
the range is in command,
and the war song cannot write its nature.

Gymnast in the Dark

Something is wrong and you don't know what it is.
The ladder to your thoughts is where you left it.
The inventory of your feelings is catalogued and stacked.
The rooftops which log your horizon at night
Billow the same smoke at morning.
Socks are in the drawer.
The bed is made.

Something is wrong and you don't know what it is.
Memories travel the same tunnel to reach you.
Voices find the same bridge to cross your empty space.
The people you know do not change
What you know about yourself.
Your shadows capture your weight.
The sun does not discriminate.

Something is wrong and you don't know what it is.
You enter every room.
You exit empty-handed.
You ask the silence to invert itself
Like a gymnast in the dark.
Your mind and your heart are one.
The body does not lie.

Something is wrong and you don't know what it is.
Light after light and you keep walking.
You turn corners and square your breath.
Night weighs the sky
As oceans scale the rain.
You are part of the universe.
The universe is at sea.

As My Brother Slept

I swam a thousand miles in my sleep.
I collapsed on the grass and started dreaming.
I was drowning above my brother's house.
I kicked the roof and asked for water.

He hugged my bones and crushed my wings.
He smiled and showed his smallest teeth.
We sat in the dollhouse of the unspoken.
We were giants gnawing at our cages.

Night pitched shadows into the old tent.
The bear with the black nose fell off the shelf.
I woke up and stroked its fur.
As my brother slept his longer leg grew longer.

I balanced the bear and made the bed.
From the chimney I crawled to the nearest cloud.
It held me for a thousand miles.
It dropped me in a public square.

On a bench I played some chess.
The man in the wheelchair won every game.
He smiled and showed all his teeth.
I bought him water and walked on home.

Sea

They say the body is a sea
of cells, dividing and conquering
the outside world. They say
the outside world is a body
of divisions and conquests
brushing up against our deep

blue skin. They say the air
holds no lies, only truths
we breathe and breathe until
we breathe no longer. They say
death holds no air only the breath
of truth that can brush

a lifetime. I began reading faces
when the book of life put me
in the shelf of my mother's arms.
Now my mother's arms are reaching
through water and time
and space.

The Lake of Memories

Voices sit
like broken chairs
in a room.

A room stands
for the ceremony
of impermanence.

Impermanence cracks
the façade
of self.

The self builds
its walls
of healing.

Healing frames
the house
of wounds.

Wounds bridge
darkness and light
over time.

Time winds through
the lake of memories
in frozen tongue.

Waiting

Even at this old age
I am not tired
Of watering the same thoughts.
Burning the same pots.
Stirring the same wounds.
Letting the same illusions heal.
Watching the rain.

Even at this old age
I am not sure
When to buy new shoes.
How much to tip the postman.
What words to speak to the bereaved.
The meaning of my dreams.
What books to read.

Even at this old age
I can go on and on
From this chair.
From that window.
Without socks.
Without god.
Full of pain.

Even at this old age
I feel younger
Than my children.
Than the buds in the trees.
Than the spring flowers in the white buckets.
Gray squirrels.
Dry kisses.

Even at this old age
I am waiting
For the evidence to present itself.
For the trial to resume.
For the letter in the mailbox.
For the summons from the foreign land.
That forecast from the sky.

Even at this old age
I want someone to tell me
Who I am.

Landscape

The man on the bench has no name.
So say the uniformed boys walking to school.
So say the pig-tailed girls skipping rope.
So say the birds who know their clientele.
So says the wind that has made its last delivery.

The man on the bench has no name.
He lost it when he dropped his keys.
He lost it when he left the house.
He lost it when someone asked him for directions.
He lost it when he fell in love.

The man on the bench has no name.
He nods a silent nod when introduced.
He smiles an old man's smile when saying goodbye.
He denies ever having had one when confronted.
He insists he doesn't want one when empathized.

The man on the bench has no name.
But he has names for the boys and the girls.
And names for their mothers and their fathers.
He even has names for the birds.
One could say he tosses names to the wind.

The man on the bench has no name.

He was born without a name.

He was conceived without a name.

He was imagined without a name.

The man on the bench will live forever.

The Floating Chair

I want to travel far
A ship without a captain
A boat without an anchor
And reach that point of intersection
Of the water and the sky
The sharpest corner of the mind
That doesn't sink
That doesn't fly
And sit in its floating chair
Without an angle to despair
The place I thought I was
The place I am right now
Imagining the collapse
Of the heavens on my brow.

Inside

Inside every man is another man
he would like to leave behind.
And so men will collect things
until they forget that they are collecting;
while young boys bide their time
near city dumps.

Inside every woman is another woman
she imagines she might have been.
And so women will rehearse roles
until they forget that they are acting;
while young girls paint lipstick
preening in their mothers' pumps.

Inside every couple is another couple
wandering the trails of another union.
And so couples will adopt other narratives
until they forget that they are drafting;
while young boys and young girls carve initials
in century-old stumps.

A Life of Carvings

The light fell down and broke
the day's façade in two.
The bigger piece unhinged
the past; the smaller piece
took the beating of the sun.
And in the mind's reflection
I was holding something larger
than the afternoon could mirror.
If I put it down as the weight
of time, dying men in half-
windowed beds rose up in laughter.
If I framed it as the quotidian,
a pregnant woman disrobed
and birthed a gaze beyond her tent.
And if I yielded to its withholding,
it simply held me without yield.
Then the night fell down
and asked me to move deeper.
Under the cover of stars
I dug shadows from my silhouette,
laying them like jewels
in the unscrolling of a will.

Every one was there: the student,
the lover, the child, the son,
the brother, the friend; the happy
man and the sad man—a life
of carvings and all the discarded
shavings. But the shadows kept
peeling layers from their kin,
too maternal to leave an imprint
for capture on the ground.
So I fell down, too, rolling
every contour of my façade
on the skin of the unknown,
as if the hands that held me
to the wind would catch me;
a pebble from a rooftop falling
on a road of pebbles
only a still pond could hear.

Insomnia

Real poets never sleep.
Theirs is a constant whisper
on a dark road long forsaken.
But in their dreams they return
to reclaim the walk
with the moon
and the deer
and the red telephone in the box.

Real poets never wake
to call on their dreams.
Not for a falling body
or an upward breeze.
Not for a whisper
between consciousness.
Nor the sound of footsteps late at night
receding into the woods.

Night & Day

A man in a room
is a house in a field.
When night falls
house and field are one;
man and room, two.
When day breaks
house and field are two;
man and room, three.

A woman in a room
is a boat on a lake.
When night falls,
boat and lake are one;
woman and moon, two.
When day breaks
boat and lake are two;
woman and moon, one.

A man and a woman in a room
is a year in a century.
When night falls
year and century are one;

man and woman and moon, a timeless century.
When day breaks
year and century are two,
man and woman and moon, one year at a time.

Perfect Faith

Feed me the perfect vision the way
a good rain feeds the grass: sleeping,
dreaming, or turning on its side

the good earth knows how to receive
when its mouth is dry, often rising
in teary applause. They say Abraham

knew how to receive too, in his tent,
full of words for generations and generations.
Yet I only recall his disquieting offering:

perfect faith. And so I wonder now
if Abraham were asked to sacrifice
the brilliant sun for the indiscriminate

rain, what instrument might he have chosen
on his walk to blind heavens' face:
a rock or a stone to still water

to erase the sky? A bow and then an
arrow—the arcs of two rainbows—man
and man-made? Perhaps old Abraham

might have fathered a small body
of water, nestled in the undulating meadow,
perfectly recording rain's bullets one piece

at a time, so that God's hearing might've
rejected the sun's appeal. Or perhaps old
Abraham would've used his naked hands,

cupped in prayer, a half-appled slice of air,
to break the covenant between two palms
of light.

Till the Apple-Pickers Come

One more poem.
One more lover.
One more touch by the signature unknown.
One more rescue in the lyrical form.

One more city.
One more language.
One more swim in the lake of the foreign.
One more escape from the stroke of the sovereign.

One more cloud.
One more thought.
One more expression of the infinite.
One more release from all the approximate.

One more sound.
One more silence.
One more hearing by the argument of denial.
One more affirmation of the human trial.

One more wave.
One more emotion.

One more breathing from the origin.
One more seeding of the being and the been.

One more blossom.
One more gesture.
One more truth for the heavenly sum.
One more one more till the apple-pickers come.

The Canvas in the Room

There is nothing to do with words today.
All words in all languages want to be left alone.
Those in books are enjoying the company of the dark.
Those about to be spoken are turning from the light.
Those that have slid from mind to heart are rolling in the mud.
Those on naked swims in pristine lakes refuse all dress.
Those on moonlit hikes in snowy fields do not want another eye.
Those on sandy beaches have embraced their tracks.

There is nothing to do with words today.
All words in all languages want to rest.
They have traveled the clouds and they have run from the gods.
They have done their immortal duty.
They have made war and they have made love.
They have killed animal and they have killed bird.
They have survived two testaments.
They have sung their song.

There is nothing to do with words today.
They will not be assembled.
They will not approach the picket line.
Foreign lands and exotic feasts offer no enticement.

They refuse to sleep and they refuse to nap.
They refuse to stand.
They have no endgame.
They are not made for man.

There is nothing to do with words today.
There was never anything to do with words.
The river never stopped for reflection.
The leaf never shrank from interpretation.
The wave never changed its mind.
The flame never asked to dance.
The sky never painted a cloud.
I am dripping in silence.

When the Ground Is Infinite

We make our peace.
When the metaphors are packed and sealed
and the sky has shipped its last cloud.
When the ground is infinite
and our pain is a stone;
and our deepest well makes a sound.

We make our peace.
When the shadows have gone far and gone wide
and the net of darkness is caught up in light.
When the horizon is a window
and our views are lifted by two hands;
and our deepest sigh makes a mark.

We make our peace.
When the days stand between two nights
and dreams sit out the stars.
When time has sifted enough falsehoods from the pile
and memory is spotted on the table;
and our imagined life makes neither mark nor sound.

ACKNOWLEDGMENTS

I am deeply grateful to Katie Hall for her meticulous reading of the poems in these pages. Hers is an intelligence brimming with secrets.

Along the way a few poems were lifted by a voice that was not my own, but one whose urgency and grace identified my voice to others; I am eternally thankful to Patricia Clarkson.

I wish to take my hat off to Adrian Dannatt.

I wish to dance a thousand dances for Jonathan Rabinowitz.

And if the sky's the limit, I'd like to tap on the names of John Ashbery, Carol Muske-Dukes, and D. Nurkse, and ask the clouds to carry their light to wishing ponds around the world.

Finally, I'd like to thank the editors of the following journals in which a number of poems in this collection first appeared: *Bomb* (online): "The Painted Room"; *The Dirty Goat*: "Salvador da Bahia," "November Wound," "Olinda"; *Inkwell*: "Shoes"; *New England Review*: "Animals"; *Open City*: "Stones," "Island," "Gymnast in the Dark," "Sunday Monday"; *Ploughshares*: "Bluebird," "In This House"; *Poetry*: "Fragments."